Gottlieb G. Huber

Narrative Coaching for Transformation and Growth

Strategies for Overcoming Challenges and Achieving Personal Excellence through Stories.

tredition

© 2024, Gottlieb G. Huber

Druck und Distribution im Auftrag des Autors/der Autorin:
tredition GmbH, Heinz-Beusen-Stieg 5, 22926 Ahrensburg, Deutschland

Das Werk, einschließlich seiner Teile, ist urheberrechtlich geschützt. Für die Inhalte ist die Autorin / der Autor verantwortlich. Jede Verwertung ist ohne ihre Zustimmung unzulässig. Die Publikation und Verbreitung erfolgen im Auftrag der Autorin, zu erreichen unter: tredition GmbH, Abteilung "Impressumservice", Heinz-Beusen-Stieg 5, 22926 Ahrensburg, Deutschland

Contents

I. Understanding Narrative Coaching 2
   Introduction to Narrative Coaching 2
      Defining Narrative Coaching and its principles 2
      Significance of storytelling in personal development 4
      Overview of narrative coaching methods 5
      Importance of narratives in shaping identity 7
   Foundations of Narrative Coaching 10
      Exploring the roots of narrative thinking 10
      Contrasting narrative coaching with traditional coaching . 12
      Techniques for incorporating stories into coaching sessions
      13

II. The Power of Storytelling in Coaching 16
   Types of Stories in Coaching 16
      Understanding different story archetypes 16
      How personal narratives influence coaching outcomes 18
      Leveraging storytelling for self-reflection and growth 20
   Crafting Compelling Narratives 21
      Strategies for developing impactful coaching stories 22
      Case studies highlighting effective storytelling techniques 24
      Engaging clients through storytelling exercises 26

III. Applying Narrative Coaching in Different Life Domains . 29
   Career Development and Narrative Coaching 29
      Integrating storytelling in career coaching sessions 29
      Case studies of successful career narrative transformations
      31
      Tools for exploring professional narratives with clients 33
   Relationship Enhancement through Narratives 34
      Utilizing stories to improve interpersonal dynamics 35
      Resolving conflicts through narrative exploration 37

Promoting empathy and understanding in relationships ...39

IV. Practical Methods and Exercises in Narrative Coaching..... 40
Interactive Techniques for Personal Growth..............................40
    Hands-on exercises for self-awareness and reflection 41
    Designing narrative-focused coaching sessions....................43
    Adapting exercises for individual client needs 45
Tools for Effective Storytelling...47
    Enhancing communication skills through storytelling........47
    Strategies for eliciting impactful client narratives 49
    Implementing storytelling techniques in coaching practice 51

V. Ethical Considerations in Narrative Coaching 53
Upholding Professional Standards..53
    Importance of ethical guidelines in coaching narratives 53
    Respecting client confidentiality and boundaries.................55
    Navigating ethical dilemmas in narrative coaching.............56
Building Trusting Client Relationships..58
    Cultivating trust through ethical coaching practices 58
    Addressing power dynamics in storytelling relationships .60
    Ensuring a safe space for sharing personal narratives.........61

VI. Advancing Skills in Narrative Coaching 64
Mastering Advanced Techniques 64
    Exploring nuanced storytelling methods................................64
    Enhancing narrative analysis skills..67
    Facilitating transformative coaching experiences.................68
Personal Development as a Narrative Coach..............................69
    Reflecting on personal growth through coaching practice..70
    Opportunities for ongoing professional development 72
    Integrating self-awareness into coaching approaches..........74

VII. Reinforcing Narrative Coaching Practices 76
Resources for Continued Learning..76
    Further training opportunities in narrative coaching 76
    Continuing education options for narrative coaches 78
    Building a supportive community of narrative coaching
    professionals 79
Future Trends in Narrative Coaching 81

Emerging developments in narrative coaching.................... 81
Innovations shaping the future of narrative coaching 84
Recommendations for staying current in the field............... 86

VIII. Concluding Thoughts and Application of Narrative Coaching.. 89
Summary of Key Insights.. 89
Recap of core concepts in narrative coaching 89
Highlights from successful narrative coaching applications 91
Key takeaways for implementing narrative coaching strategies 93
Encouragement for Practical Implementation.......................... 95
Motivation to apply narrative coaching techniques 96
Actionable steps for incorporating storytelling into coaching practice 98
Inspiring clients towards personal growth and transformation... 101

IX. Supplemental Materials and Resources............................ 103
Glossary of Essential Terms 103
Definition and explanation of key narrative coaching terms 103
Clarifying terminology for effective communication in coaching 105
Enhancing understanding through a comprehensive glossary 107
Further Reading and Professional Networks 109
Recommending additional resources for in-depth learning 110
Directory of coaching associations and organizations 112
Building connections within the narrative coaching community... 114

I. Understanding Narrative Coaching

Introduction to Narrative Coaching

As human beings, we are constantly weaving our stories, shaping our identities through the narratives we tell ourselves and others. In this section, we will delve into the intricate relationship between storytelling and personal identity, exploring how the stories we create influence who we are and who we become. From understanding the role of narratives in identity formation to examining the impact of life events on our stories, we will uncover the transformative power of narrative coaching in shaping our identities for personal growth and development. Join us on this journey of self-discovery as we explore the profound connection between narratives and personal identity.

Defining Narrative Coaching and its principles

Narrative Coaching, a transformative approach to personal development, centers on harnessing the power of storytelling to evoke change. At its core, this practice delves into the intricate relationship between stories and personal growth, emphasizing narratives as pivotal tools for self-reflection, identity formation, and addressing challenges. The fundamental principles that guide Narrative Coaching underscore the significance of narrative thinking and its ability to uncover deep-seated beliefs and patterns, distinguishing it from traditional coaching methods.

One of the primary distinctions of Narrative Coaching lies in its utilization of stories as a means to explore clients' inner worlds, promote introspection, and foster understanding and empathy. By engaging with clients' narratives, coaches can help individuals reframe their experiences, challenge limiting beliefs, and envision new possibilities for their future. This approach is particularly effective in various life domains, including career transitions, relationship dynamics, health challenges, and personal growth journeys.

Ethical considerations are paramount in Narrative Coaching, ensuring that coaches uphold professional standards, respect clients' confidentiality, and create a safe space for sharing personal stories. This commitment to ethical practice underpins the trust and rapport essential for meaningful coaching relationships.

Ultimately, the impact of Narrative Coaching extends far beyond mere self-improvement, often leading to profound shifts in perspectives, personal agency, and emotional well-being. By guiding individuals through the process of rewriting their narratives, this coaching style catalyzes deep-rooted transformation and empowers clients to embrace new narratives that align with their aspirations and values.

Significance of storytelling in personal development

Stories play a profound role in defining individuals' identities, serving as a mirror through which they perceive themselves and their place in the world. These narratives shape beliefs, values, and behaviors, influencing how individuals see themselves and are seen by others. In the realm of problem-solving, stories offer a unique perspective by reframing challenges, providing insights from past experiences, and inspiring innovative solutions. By leveraging the power of storytelling, individuals can navigate obstacles with creativity and resilience.

The mechanism behind narrative change lies in the transformative potential of stories to inspire personal growth and development. Through reflection on past experiences, reevaluation of beliefs, and the construction of new narratives, individuals can rewrite their stories, identifying patterns, and creating pathways for positive change. In the context of coaching, storytelling techniques enhance professional outcomes by deepening the coaching relationship, fostering empathy, and promoting self-awareness. Coaches adept in storytelling can guide clients through a journey of self-discovery, facilitating meaningful shifts in perspective and behavior.

Ethical considerations are paramount in storytelling within coaching practices. Coaches must honor the confidentiality and trust of clients, handling personal narratives with sensitivity and respect. By upholding ethical standards, coaches can create a safe and supportive space for clients to explore and share their stories, fostering a foundation of trust essential for transformative coaching experiences.

Overview of narrative coaching methods

Narrative Coaching methods serve as a powerful tool in facilitating personal development through the use of narrative-based techniques. Central to this approach is the process of identifying and extracting stories that individuals carry within them. By delving into these narratives, clients can gain insights into their own experiences, beliefs, and identity constructs. Coaches, employing reflexivity and active listening, provide a supportive environment for clients to explore these narratives, assisting them in understanding and reshaping their life stories towards positive change.

Moreover, coaches guide clients in recognizing and applying narrative patterns, helping them navigate through challenges and envision new possibilities. By teaching clients to harness the power of storytelling, coaches enable individuals to construct empowering narratives that align with their aspirations and values. The use of metaphors in coaching further enhances this process, allowing for the expression of complex emotions and experiences in a more accessible and impactful manner.

In essence, Narrative Coaching not only emphasizes the importance of stories in personal growth but also equips individuals with the tools to rewrite their narratives, fostering self-discovery and transformation.

Importance of narratives in shaping identity

Defining Personal Identity:

Personal identity is a complex amalgam of traits, beliefs, values, and experiences that distinguish one individual from another. It encompasses the essence of who we are, our self-perception, and how we relate to the world. Factors contributing to an individual's identity include genetic makeup, cultural background, societal influences, personal experiences, and relationships with others. Our identity is not static; it evolves over time as we navigate life's experiences and challenges.

Interplay Between Narratives and Identity Formation:

The stories we tell about ourselves play a crucial role in shaping our personal identities. These narratives reflect our self-perceptions, beliefs, values, and understanding of the world. Through storytelling, individuals make sense of their experiences, construct meaning, and reinforce or challenge their identities. The narratives we internalize can either empower us to embrace our true selves or limit our potential for growth and change.

Impact of Life Events on Narratives:

Major life events such as career transitions, relationship changes, loss, or personal achievements have the power to reshape our personal narratives. These events can challenge existing beliefs, values, and self-perceptions, leading to a reevaluation of who we are and what we stand for. How we interpret and make sense of these life events through our narratives can profoundly influence our identity development and growth.

Narrative Identity Theory Introduction:

Narrative identity theory suggests that individuals construct their identities through the stories they tell about themselves. According to this theory, our personal narratives form the foundation of our self-concept and guide our actions, decisions, and relationships. By examining the themes, characters, and plotlines of our life stories, we can gain insight into our deepest desires, fears, and aspirations, leading to a deeper understanding of ourselves and our place in the world.

Identity Change Through Narrative Revision:

The process of altering our personal narratives can catalyze profound transformations in our identities. By revisiting and revising the stories we tell about ourselves, we can challenge limiting beliefs, overcome internalized obstacles, and envision new possibilities for personal growth and self-realization. Through narrative revision, individuals have the opportunity to rewrite their life scripts, embrace new identities, and cultivate a greater sense of authenticity and agency in their lives.

Role of Narrative Coaching in Shaping Identity:

Narrative coaching offers a unique approach to facilitating positive identity transformations by leveraging the power of storytelling and self-reflection. Through guided exploration of personal narratives, individuals can uncover hidden patterns, uncover deep-seated beliefs, and reimagine their life stories in empowering and liberating ways. Narrative coaching techniques such as deep listening, reframing, metaphorical exploration, and narrative reconstruction can help clients gain clarity, insight, and agency in reshaping their identities, overcoming obstacles, and embracing their full potential. By harnessing the transformative potential of storytelling, narrative coaching empowers individuals to rewrite their life narratives, cultivate resilience, and embark on a journey of self-discovery and personal growth.

Foundations of Narrative Coaching

Embarking on a journey through the intricate realm of narrative thinking opens up a doorway to the fascinating origins and evolution of how stories shape our understanding of the world. From the methods employed by early societies to the modern applications that impact personal growth, narrative thinking serves as a powerful tool for self-reflection and transformation. As we delve into the intricate web of personal narratives and storytelling, we uncover the profound impact they have on the coaching process, guiding individuals towards deeper insights and self-discovery. Join us as we explore the role of stories in coaching, and unravel the unique benefits that narrative coaching brings to the table.

Exploring the roots of narrative thinking

Narrative thinking, originating in early human societies, emerged as a fundamental cognitive process deeply embedded in the human psyche. Early societies relied on storytelling not only for communication but also for transferring knowledge, values, and cultural practices across generations. Over time, narrative thinking evolved into a sophisticated mechanism for making sense of the world and shaping personal and collective identities.

The history and evolution of narrative thinking have been studied extensively, revealing its multifaceted nature and significance. Research delves into how narratives construct reality, influence decision-making, and foster connections between individuals and communities. Various studies have explored the psychological, social, and even neurological underpinnings of narrative thinking, highlighting its role in shaping beliefs, attitudes, and behaviors.

Modern applications of narrative thinking span diverse fields, including psychology, literature, marketing, and beyond. In therapy and coaching, for instance, individuals harness the power of storytelling to gain insights into their experiences, reframe perspectives, and facilitate personal growth. The impact of narrative thinking on personal development is profound, emphasizing the transformative potential of understanding and reshaping one's own narrative. By engaging in reflective storytelling, individuals can navigate challenges, foster resilience, and cultivate a deeper sense of self-awareness and well-being.

Contrasting narrative coaching with traditional coaching

Traditional coaching, rooted in goal-setting and performance enhancement, navigates clients through achieving measurable outcomes by employing techniques like inquiry, feedback, and action plans. This structured methodology prioritizes results-driven processes and skill development within a predefined framework.

In contrast, narrative coaching delves deeper into individuals' stories, beliefs, and values to foster personal growth and transformation. By recognizing the narratives that shape one's identity and challenges, clients can rewrite their stories, leading to profound shifts in behavior and perspective. This approach emphasizes self-reflection and understanding, aiming to transform not only behaviors but also the core narratives guiding those behaviors.

The fundamental difference between these coaching methodologies lies in their focus: traditional coaching centers on external objectives, while narrative coaching centers on inner exploration and self-awareness. Narrative coaching's unique benefit lies in its ability to unearth deeply ingrained thought patterns and emotional triggers that traditional coaching might overlook.

To illustrate, while a traditional coach might work with a client to set specific career goals, a narrative coach could explore the underlying stories and beliefs influencing the client's career choices and aspirations, resulting in a more transformative and holistic approach to personal development and change.

Techniques for incorporating stories into coaching sessions

Stories are integral to the coaching process, acting as powerful tools for self-discovery and growth. Personal narratives shape an individual's identity, beliefs, and behaviors, influencing how they perceive themselves and the world around them. In coaching, uncovering and understanding these narratives are fundamental to supporting clients in overcoming obstacles, setting goals, and making positive changes in their lives.

Using storytelling in coaching sessions provides a platform for clients to articulate their experiences, emotions, and desires. Through storytelling, clients gain clarity on their values, motivations, and aspirations, fostering self-awareness and encouraging introspection. Coaches can leverage these narratives to facilitate deeper conversations, challenge limiting beliefs, and inspire personal transformation.

When incorporating stories for personal development, individuals have the opportunity to revisit and re-evaluate their narratives. By reframing past experiences and reinterpreting their significance, clients can gain new perspectives, identify growth opportunities, and enhance their self-concept. This process enables clients to break free from self-imposed limitations, cultivate resilience, and envision a more fulfilling future.

Ensuring ethical storytelling practices is essential in coaching, emphasizing the importance of confidentiality, respect, and integrity in sharing personal narratives. Coaches must create a safe and supportive environment where clients feel comfortable exploring their stories without fear of judgment or breach of privacy.

Stories serve as powerful vehicles for self-exploration, empowerment, and personal growth in coaching. By harnessing the transformative potential of storytelling, both coaches and clients can embark on a journey of discovery, insight, and positive change.

II. The Power of Storytelling in Coaching

Types of Stories in Coaching

Embarking on a journey through the realms of storytelling, this section delves into the intricate world of story archetypes. From defining the essence of an archetypal story to exploring their applications in coaching practice, we unravel the significance of these timeless narratives. Join us as we navigate through the role of personal narratives in shaping self-perception, goal setting, emotional regulation, and behavior change. Discover the transformative potential of re-authored stories and the ethical considerations in self-narrative exploration. Through self-reflection and narrative immersion, we uncover the power of storytelling for growth and introspection. Welcome to a world where stories shape destinies and unlock the depths of human experience.

Understanding different story archetypes

An archetypal story serves as a foundational narrative structure that transcends cultural boundaries and resonates universally. Within the realm of narrative coaching, these stories provide a rich tapestry of themes and characters that hold significance for personal development and change. Common story archetypes frequently encountered in narrative coaching include the Hero's Journey, where an individual embarks on a transformative quest; the Mentor, who offers guidance and wisdom; the Shadow, representing repressed or ignored aspects of the self; and the Trickster, embodying unpredictability and change.

Story archetypes become invaluable tools in coaching practice as they serve as mirrors for clients, reflecting their internal narratives and external challenges. By recognizing and working with these archetypes, coaches can help clients navigate their identity formation, address obstacles, and facilitate growth. Through a deeper exploration of the roles these archetypes play in client narratives, coaches can assist individuals in reshaping their stories and fostering self-awareness.

In essence, story archetypes offer a powerful lens through which clients can perceive their experiences and aspirations. By leveraging these archetypes within coaching sessions, coaches can foster introspection, encourage transformative insights, and guide clients towards personal evolution. Hence, recognizing, understanding, and applying story archetypes in narrative coaching practice can profoundly impact clients' journeys toward self-discovery and positive change.

How personal narratives influence coaching outcomes

Personal narratives are not just stories we tell about ourselves; they are powerful tools that shape how we view ourselves and interact with the world. These narratives influence our self-perception by reflecting back our beliefs, values, and experiences, which in turn impact our confidence, resilience, and overall well-being. When individuals consciously examine and reframe their personal stories, they can challenge and transform limiting beliefs, allowing for a more empowering self-concept.

In the realm of goal setting, personal narratives provide a roadmap for aligning aspirations with one's core values and identity. By crafting goals that resonate with their story, individuals are more likely to stay motivated and committed throughout the journey. The coherence between personal narratives and goals creates a sense of purpose and direction that propels individuals forward even in the face of challenges.

Emotional regulation is another realm where personal narratives play a significant role. By narrating our emotional experiences and understanding the stories behind our feelings, individuals can cultivate emotional intelligence and resilience. By recognizing patterns in their narratives, individuals can learn to regulate emotions effectively, leading to greater emotional well-being.

When it comes to behavior change, personal narratives can be both enablers and inhibitors. By reshaping the stories we tell about ourselves and our capabilities, individuals can shift their mindset and behaviors towards positive change. Understanding the underlying stories that drive behaviors allows individuals to make intentional choices and break free from self-limiting patterns.

In conflict resolution, personal narratives are key to fostering understanding and empathy. By sharing and listening to each other's stories, conflicting parties can uncover common ground, humanize each other's perspectives, and find resolutions that honor the complexity of their narratives. Through storytelling, individuals can bridge differences, build trust, and move towards reconciliation and collaboration.

Personal narratives are at the heart of our identity, motivation, emotional well-being, behavior, and relationships. By exploring and reshaping these narratives, individuals can unlock their potential for growth, self-awareness, and meaningful connections with others.

Leveraging storytelling for self-reflection and growth

Self-reflection in storytelling is a powerful tool for personal growth and development. By delving into narratives, individuals can explore their experiences, emotions, and beliefs in a structured and reflective manner. Techniques such as journaling, storytelling prompts, or even creating fictional characters can provide frameworks for introspection and growth.

Narrative immersion plays a crucial role in this process, allowing individuals to immerse themselves in different perspectives and viewpoints. This immersion enables a deeper understanding of one's own narrative and can lead to profound insights and self-discovery.

Through the use of self-narratives, individuals can identify and address barriers that may be hindering their personal growth. This can include recognizing and challenging self-limiting beliefs, exploring past traumas, or understanding recurring patterns in one's life.

The transformative potential of re-authored stories is significant. By reframing and rewriting personal narratives, individuals can shift their perspectives, create new meanings, and envision alternative futures for themselves.

However, it is essential to consider ethical considerations in self-narrative exploration. Respecting privacy, ensuring consent when sharing personal stories, and maintaining confidentiality are paramount in this process to create a safe and supportive environment for self-reflection and growth.

Crafting Compelling Narratives

Exploring the Depths of Client Stories

Within the realm of narrative coaching, the power of storytelling is unparalleled. As coaches, it is crucial to be able to unravel the depths of our clients' stories, understanding their context, key messages, and emotional connections. In this section, we will delve into the intricacies of client case studies, clarifying their purpose and exploring effective techniques for eliciting and creating impactful stories. Through reflective listening and analysis, we will uncover the outcomes and transformations that can arise from these storytelling exercises. Join us as we navigate the rich landscape of our clients' stories, acknowledging their uniqueness and guiding them towards self-discovery and growth.

Strategies for developing impactful coaching stories

Understanding the client's context in Narrative Coaching is a multifaceted process that involves unraveling the key message embedded within their stories. This entails actively listening to not just what is said but also what is implied, helping the coach gain a deeper understanding of the client's underlying beliefs, values, and perspectives. By doing so, the coach can identify recurring themes, conflicts, and emotional nuances that shape the client's narrative.

Creating emotional connections with the client's story is crucial in building rapport and trust. It involves empathizing with the client's experiences, validating their emotions, and offering a supportive space for reflection and exploration. This emotional resonance can facilitate a deeper engagement with the coaching process, enabling the client to share more authentically and work through challenges effectively.

Intertwining the client's personal experiences within the narrative is a powerful technique that allows for a holistic understanding of their journey. By connecting past experiences, present circumstances, and future aspirations, the client can gain clarity on their identity, goals, and desired changes. This approach also helps in identifying patterns, triggers, and opportunities for growth and transformation.

Exploring symbolic elements within the client's stories reveals hidden meanings and subconscious associations that may hold significant insights for personal development. Symbolism can represent deep-seated emotions, desires, fears, and aspirations that the client may not be consciously aware of. By unpacking these symbols with the client, the coach can uncover layers of meaning, facilitate self-discovery, and catalyze transformative change.

Utilizing literary techniques such as metaphor, imagery, and dialogue enhances the storytelling process in coaching. Metaphors can provide fresh perspectives and reframes, allowing the client to see their situation from a new angle. Imagery helps evoke sensory experiences and emotional responses, making the narrative more vivid and engaging. Dialogue, whether internal or external, can prompt self-reflection, challenge limiting beliefs, and foster insights that propel personal growth.

Overall, understanding the client's context through unraveling the key message, creating emotional connections, intertwining personal experiences, exploring symbolic elements, and utilizing literary techniques is essential for effective Narrative Coaching. It enables the coach to guide clients towards self-awareness, empowerment, and positive change through the transformative power of storytelling.

Case studies highlighting effective storytelling techniques

Case studies play a pivotal role in the realm of Narrative Coaching, offering concrete examples that showcase the practical application of coaching techniques in diverse scenarios. These real-life narratives serve a dual purpose: they provide coaches with insightful illustrations of how specific strategies can be implemented to address varied challenges, and they offer clients a mirror through which they can reflect on their own experiences and potential paths of growth.

Effective story elicitation techniques are central to the process of uncovering these narratives. Coaches employ a blend of empathetic listening, skillful questioning, and creating a non-judgmental environment to encourage clients to share their stories openly and authentically. This approach not only helps in understanding the clients' perspectives but also forms the foundation upon which subsequent coaching interventions can be built.

Similarly, effective story creation techniques are crucial for guiding clients in reshaping their narratives towards positive change and personal growth. Coaches assist individuals in reframing their stories, exploring alternative perspectives, and envisioning new possibilities. These techniques empower clients to harness the transformative potential of their own narratives, fostering self-awareness and facilitating the process of change.

Reflective listening is a cornerstone skill in Narrative Coaching, wherein coaches actively listen to clients' stories, reflect back key themes, emotions, and experiences, and validate the clients' perspectives. Through reflective listening, coaches not only demonstrate empathy and understanding but also help clients explore their narratives more deeply, fostering a sense of connection and trust within the coaching relationship.

By delving into case studies and analyzing outcomes and transformations, coaches can glean valuable insights into the efficacy of Narrative Coaching techniques. Through these detailed examinations, coaches can ascertain the impact of narrative interventions on clients' personal development and change processes. Each case study offers a unique narrative that exemplifies the power of storytelling in fostering self-discovery, resilience, and growth within the coaching journey.

Engaging clients through storytelling exercises

In the realm of narrative coaching, a crucial aspect lies in comprehending the landscape of a client's story. Each individual's narrative holds a unique essence, reflecting their experiences, beliefs, and aspirations. Recognizing this intrinsic diversity is paramount in cultivating a coaching environment that resonates with the client on a personal level. When selecting storytelling exercises, it is essential to carefully consider the client's story type and specific requirements. Tailoring exercises to align with the client's needs can enhance the efficacy of the coaching process, fostering a deeper connection between the narratives shared and the client's personal journey.

Implementing storytelling exercises requires a structured methodology while allowing for authentic expression from the client. By creating a safe space for clients to explore and articulate their stories, coaches can encourage self-reflection and facilitate meaningful personal growth. Active client engagement is pivotal in this process. Employing strategies that prompt participation and involvement in storytelling activities can deepen the impact of the coaching experience.

Monitoring client progress involves a meticulous evaluation of the advancements in self-reflection and personal development. Tracking these changes provides valuable insights into the client's evolving narrative and growth trajectory. Throughout these exercises, upholding ethical standards is paramount. Safeguarding client confidentiality and demonstrating unwavering respect for their stories are non-negotiable aspects of practicing narrative coaching. By prioritizing these ethical considerations, coaches can cultivate a trusting and conducive environment for transformative storytelling experiences.

III. Applying Narrative Coaching in Different Life Domains

Career Development and Narrative Coaching

Embarking on a journey through the intricate world of career narratives, we delve into the power of storytelling in shaping career-related decisions. From understanding the significance of clients' career narratives to utilizing them for career mapping, we navigate through techniques that elicit in-depth stories and promote self-reflection. Through detailed analysis of case studies and professional narratives, we explore the concept of narrative identity in the workplace and the ethical considerations that come into play. Join us as we uncover the transformative potential of storytelling in career development.

Integrating storytelling in career coaching sessions

Stories play a vital role in the realm of career development, acting as powerful tools that influence individuals' decision-making processes, aspirations, and self-perceptions. As Narrative Coaches delve into clients' career narratives, they uncover multifaceted layers of experiences, beliefs, and motivations that shape professional paths. Techniques such as active listening, probing questions, and reflection enable coaches to elicit detailed career stories from clients, offering a deeper understanding of their challenges, successes, and goals.

By harnessing these narratives for career mapping, coaches guide clients in exploring potential trajectories that resonate with their authentic selves. Analyzing and revising career stories becomes a pivotal step, prompting clients to reflect on patterns, overcome obstacles, and craft narratives that align with their envisioned futures. Through this process, clients gain insights into their strengths, values, and areas for growth, leading to empowered career decision-making and advancement.

Moreover, storytelling in career coaching serves as a catalyst for self-reflection, fostering personal growth and professional development. As clients engage with their career stories, they confront pivotal moments, setbacks, and triumphs, thereby gaining clarity on their identities and aspirations. This reflective process not only enhances self-awareness but also cultivates resilience and adaptability in navigating career transitions.

Ethics form the cornerstone of Narrative Career Coaching, guiding coaches in upholding confidentiality, respect, and integrity while engaging with clients' personal narratives. By maintaining a professional and empathetic stance, coaches create a safe space for clients to share candidly, fostering trust and collaboration in the coaching partnership. Through this ethical lens, coaches honor clients' stories, harnessing their transformative potential for meaningful career exploration and growth.

Case studies of successful career narrative transformations

Career narrative cases provide rich and illuminating insights into individuals' professional trajectories, shedding light on their decisions, challenges, and successes. In the chosen case studies, we examine two distinct yet equally compelling stories of career evolution.

In Case Study One, we follow Maria, a corporate professional who embarks on the challenging journey of transitioning to entrepreneurship. Through a detailed analysis of Maria's narrative, we uncover the intricate web of motivations, fears, and aspirations that accompanied her decision. By delving deeply into Maria's experiences, we gain valuable insights into the pivotal role of passion, resilience, and strategic planning in navigating significant career shifts. Moreover, Maria's story serves as a testament to the transformative power of embracing risks and learning from setbacks as integral parts of the career development process.

Turning to Case Study Two, we explore David's remarkable transition from a successful finance career to a leadership role in the nonprofit sector. Through a nuanced examination of David's journey, we unravel the layers of introspection, perseverance, and community support that fueled his professional reinvention. By engaging with David's experiences, we unearth essential lessons on the importance of values alignment, continual learning, and meaningful connections in fostering career growth and fulfillment. David's story exemplifies the profound impact of self-awareness, networking, and purpose-driven decision-making in shaping one's career trajectory.

In synthesizing the detailed analysis of these two case studies, we glean a wealth of key learnings and actionable insights that can inform and inspire individuals navigating their own career transitions. Each narrative underscores the significance of personal agency, adaptability, and resilience in forging a fulfilling and purposeful professional path. By immersing ourselves in Maria and David's stories, we not only gain a deeper appreciation for the complexities of career development but also glean invaluable wisdom that can guide us on our own journey towards realizing our fullest potential in the professional sphere.

Tools for exploring professional narratives with clients

In the context of professional narratives, the concept of narrative identity in the workplace delves into the stories individuals construct about themselves within their professional settings. These stories encapsulate experiences, values, and aspirations that shape their perceptions of work, colleagues, and themselves as professionals. Story elicitation techniques serve as tools for coaches to uncover these narratives, prompting individuals to reflect on pivotal moments, challenges, and achievements that have influenced their career trajectory.

By analyzing professional narratives, coaches gain insight into the underlying beliefs, attitudes, and barriers that may impact an individual's performance and satisfaction in their role. This deep understanding enables targeted interventions and strategies to facilitate personal and professional growth. Applying narrative change techniques involves guiding individuals in revisiting and reframing their stories, fostering adaptations in perceptions and behaviors that align more effectively with their goals and values.

Ethical considerations are paramount in this process, emphasizing the importance of confidentiality, sensitivity, and respect for the individual's autonomy in shaping and sharing their narrative. By integrating these elements effectively, coaches empower professionals to leverage their narratives as tools for self-awareness, resilience, and adaptability in navigating the complexities of the modern workplace.

Relationship Enhancement through Narratives

Navigating relationships can be a complex and ever-evolving journey. In this section, we delve into the profound impact of empathy and understanding in fostering healthy and meaningful connections.

Through the power of stories, we explore how narratives can serve as a bridge to better comprehend and navigate relationship dynamics. Join us as we uncover the role of narrative empathy and ethical practices in building stronger and more fulfilling relationships.

Utilizing stories to improve interpersonal dynamics

Interpersonal dynamics, the complex interplay of behaviors, emotions, and communication patterns within relationships, are often illuminated through the lens of storytelling. In the realm of narrative coaching, stories serve as potent vehicles for unveiling the intricate tapestry of these dynamics. When individuals recount their experiences within relationships, they offer valuable insights into their perceptions, beliefs, and values.

Understanding the role of stories in relationships involves recognizing the power of narrative in shaping our sense of self and others. By exploring and dissecting these stories, individuals can discern recurring themes, triggers, and patterns that influence their interactions. This process enables individuals to gain deeper awareness of their relational dynamics and the underlying factors that drive their behaviors.

To extract relevant relationship stories effectively, narrative coaches employ attentive listening, reflective questioning, and empathetic engagement. By encouraging clients to articulate their narratives, coaches can help them identify key themes, emotional triggers, and communication patterns that define their relationships. This introspective journey allows individuals to gain clarity on their roles within these dynamics and recognize areas for growth and change.

Harnessing narrative techniques in amending interpersonal dynamics involves assisting clients in reframing their stories, exploring alternative perspectives, and co-creating new narratives that empower them to navigate relationships more intentionally. Through this collaborative process, individuals can reframe negative narratives, challenge limiting beliefs, and develop healthier approaches to communication and conflict resolution.

Integrating ethical practices in narrative coaching for relationships is paramount to fostering a safe and supportive coaching environment. Coaches must uphold confidentiality, respect clients' autonomy, and establish clear boundaries to ensure the trust and well-being of those they serve. By adhering to ethical guidelines and promoting clients' self-determination, coaches can facilitate meaningful and transformative journeys towards healthier and more fulfilling relationships.

Resolving conflicts through narrative exploration

In Narrative Coaching, identifying problematic narratives is a nuanced process that requires the skillful use of questioning techniques. Coaches employ various questioning methods to help clients delve deeper into their stories, revealing conflicting narratives that might be holding them back or causing tension in their lives. By encouraging clients to explore different perspectives and challenge their existing beliefs, coaches can assist in uncovering hidden conflicts within the narratives that clients construct about themselves and their experiences.

Moreover, the process of building empathy through shared narratives is a powerful tool in narrative coaching. By facilitating the exploration and understanding of each other's stories, individuals can develop a sense of connection and empathy towards one another. This shared narrative experience can help bridge gaps in understanding and lead to more harmonious relationships and environments.

Reshaping personal narratives is another key aspect of narrative coaching, particularly in the context of conflict resolution. By assisting clients in reframing their narratives, coaches can help them view conflicts from new angles, leading to the potential resolution of issues and the cultivation of healthier perspectives and behaviors. Action-based narratives play a pivotal role in conflict resolution by guiding clients to envision and implement actionable steps toward resolving conflicts. By engaging in this process, clients can move from a state of conflict to one of resolution and growth.

Reflecting on resolved conflicts is an essential part of the narrative coaching journey. By encouraging clients to reflect on their experiences and learn from them, coaches promote self-awareness and personal growth. Through this reflection, individuals can gain valuable insights into how their narratives shape their interactions and relationships, empowering them to make positive changes moving forward.

By effectively utilizing questioning techniques, building empathy through shared narratives, reshaping personal narratives, incorporating action-based narratives for conflict resolution, and encouraging reflection on resolved conflicts, narrative coaching can facilitate profound personal development and positive change in clients' lives.

Promoting empathy and understanding in relationships

In the realm of Narrative Coaching, the significance of empathy and understanding cannot be overstated. These essential components form the bedrock upon which effective coaching relationships are built. Through the lens of Narrative Empathy, coaches are able to traverse the complexities of human experiences, engaging with clients on a deeply personal level. By utilizing stories as a powerful tool for understanding, coaches can delve into the narratives that shape clients' identities, beliefs, and aspirations.

Empathy, when cultivated through coaching techniques such as active listening, mirroring, and validation, becomes a transformative force that bridges the gap between coach and client. This empathic connection creates a safe space for clients to explore their stories, unpack their challenges, and envision possibilities for change and growth.

However, it is imperative for coaches to uphold ethical standards when practicing empathy. Respecting clients' emotions, boundaries, and confidentiality is paramount in fostering a trusting and respectful coaching environment. By integrating empathy into practical coaching scenarios, coaches can support clients in navigating transitions, embracing personal insights, and catalyzing meaningful transformations across various aspects of their lives.

Ultimately, empathy serves as a guiding light in the coaching journey, illuminating the path towards deeper self-awareness, connection, and empowerment for both clients and coaches alike.

IV. Practical Methods and Exercises in Narrative Coaching

Interactive Techniques for Personal Growth

Embarking on a journey of self-discovery through narrative coaching involves delving deep into one's own story. As we explore the significance of reflection in this process, we uncover the intricate relationship between self-awareness and storytelling. Through various approaches to self-reflection exercises, we pave the way for creating our personal narratives and reshaping our perspectives. This section delves into the art of identifying the narrative needs of our clients, setting session goals, and implementing interactive storytelling techniques to foster client engagement. We also delve into the importance of understanding each client's unique needs, adapting exercises to suit their situation, and maintaining ethical boundaries throughout the coaching journey. Join us on this transformative path as we navigate the terrain of self-awareness and narrative coaching.

Hands-on exercises for self-awareness and reflection

Self-awareness, a cornerstone in personal development, takes on heightened significance in Narrative Coaching due to its ability to cultivate self-understanding and facilitate transformative change through introspection. As individuals delve into their personal stories, they embark on a journey of self-discovery where reflective practices play a crucial role. By embracing self-awareness, individuals can confront their values, beliefs, and behaviors, paving the way for profound insights and growth.

The relationship between self-awareness and storytelling is intricate, with narratives serving as mirrors that reflect our inner selves. Through storytelling, individuals unravel the layers of their experiences, emotions, and perceptions, thus gaining clarity on their identity and aspirations. This process of narrative exploration invites individuals to confront their vulnerabilities, strengths, and areas for growth, fostering a deeper sense of self-awareness.

Various approaches to self-reflection exercises, including journaling, meditation, and visualization techniques, offer avenues for individuals to engage in introspection and deepen their self-awareness. By immersing themselves in these practices, individuals can uncover hidden motivations, challenge limiting beliefs, and align their actions with their values.

Creating a personal narrative involves weaving together one's life experiences, beliefs, and aspirations into a coherent story that reflects their authentic self. This narrative serves as a compass, guiding individuals towards self-acceptance, personal growth, and fulfillment. Additionally, narrative reinterpretation empowers individuals to reframe their stories, altering their perspectives and reshaping their interpretations of past experiences. By viewing their narratives through a new lens, individuals can foster resilience, cultivate optimism, and embrace change with a sense of agency and purpose.

Designing narrative-focused coaching sessions

Identifying the narrative needs of a client is essential in Narrative Coaching. This process involves attentive listening, observation, and exploration of the client's verbal and non-verbal cues to uncover underlying themes and patterns within their stories. By identifying these narrative needs, coaches can gain valuable insights into the client's beliefs, values, and motivations, which can guide the coaching process.

Once the narrative needs are identified, the next step involves formulating session goals that are in alignment with the client's narratives. These goals should be specific, measurable, achievable, relevant, and time-bound to provide a clear direction for the coaching journey. By tying session goals to the client's narratives, coaches can create a sense of coherence and purpose for the client, enhancing their motivation and commitment to the coaching process.

The sequence of storytelling techniques in a coaching session typically involves several stages. Coaches may begin by inviting the client to share their narratives, followed by engaging in reflective questioning to deepen the exploration of these stories. Co-creating new narratives with the client can be a powerful way to catalyze personal insight and transformation. By guiding the client through a process of reframing their narratives, coaches can help them discover new perspectives and possibilities for change.

Implementing interactive approaches for client engagement is vital in Narrative Coaching. These approaches can include role-playing exercises, visualization techniques, storytelling prompts, and other creative activities that encourage active participation and deepen the client's engagement with their narratives. By incorporating interactive elements into the coaching process, coaches can enhance the client's self-awareness, creativity, and problem-solving skills.

Evaluating the effectiveness of storytelling techniques during the session is crucial for monitoring progress and adapting the coaching approach as needed. Coaches can assess the impact of storytelling techniques by observing the client's reactions, listening to their insights, and tracking changes in their narratives over time. By regularly evaluating the effectiveness of these techniques, coaches can ensure that the coaching process remains focused, relevant, and beneficial for the client.

Deciding on session termination involves determining when the client has achieved their goals and made significant progress in their personal development. Coaches should collaboratively review the client's narratives, reflect on the milestones achieved, and assess the fulfillment of session goals. By summarizing the client's progress and celebrating their achievements, coaches can provide closure to the coaching relationship and empower the client to continue their journey of growth and change.

Adapting exercises for individual client needs

When understanding a client's unique needs in narrative coaching, it is essential to personalize exercise selection to resonate with and suit their specific situation. By tailoring activities to the individual, the coaching process becomes more effective and meaningful. Consideration of the client's readiness levels is crucial in guiding them through their personal development journey. Being attuned to where they are in their growth allows for a more targeted and supportive approach.

Maintaining flexibility in methods is key as clients evolve during the coaching process. Being adaptable and willing to modify approaches ensures that the coaching remains relevant and beneficial as the client progresses. Regularly evaluating the impact of adapted exercises on the client's transformation is vital for tracking their growth and making necessary adjustments.

Furthermore, ethics play a significant role in adapting exercises. It is essential to ensure that any modifications made respect the client's boundaries and maintain strict confidentiality. Upholding ethical standards in adapting exercises not only fosters trust and respect within the coaching relationship but also safeguards the client's well-being throughout the coaching journey. By prioritizing personalization, readiness levels, flexibility, evaluation, and ethical considerations in exercise adaptation, narrative coaches can effectively meet their clients' unique needs and facilitate genuine personal development and change.

Tools for Effective Storytelling

Embarking on a journey through the art of storytelling, this section delves into the intricate details of crafting compelling narratives. From understanding the role of storytelling in communication to exploring the importance of active listening and emotional resonance, each chapter is designed to equip you with the tools necessary to captivate any audience. Get ready to discover how storytelling can inspire change and create a lasting impact in any client context.

Enhancing communication skills through storytelling

Crafting effective stories is a skill that requires a structurally sound narrative with a cohesive flow to captivate and engage the audience. Within this structure, a story typically consists of essential elements like a beginning, middle, and end, which create a framework for the plot development. The structure ensures that the story unfolds logically, maintaining the audience's interest and guiding them through the narrative journey smoothly.

Active listening is a key component in storytelling as it allows the storyteller to gauge the audience's reactions and adjust the story accordingly. By actively listening to verbal and non-verbal cues, the storyteller can tailor their narrative to the audience's preferences and emotional responses, enhancing the overall storytelling experience.

Utilizing emotional resonance in storytelling is a powerful technique to create a connection between the storyteller and the audience. Emotions are a universal language that can evoke empathy, understanding, and engagement, enabling the audience to relate to the story on a personal level. By infusing emotion into the narrative, the storyteller can make the story more memorable and impactful.

Adapting stories to various audience types is essential to ensure that the message resonates with different individuals. Understanding the audience's demographics, interests, and cultural background allows the storyteller to customize the story to suit the audience's preferences. This adaptability enhances the story's relevance and relatability, making it more compelling and effective in conveying its intended message.

Storytelling serves as a powerful tool for inspiring change by compelling individuals to reflect on their beliefs, values, and behaviors. Through storytelling, complex ideas and concepts can be communicated in a compelling and accessible manner, inspiring the audience to reexamine their perspectives and take action towards personal growth and transformation. The emotional impact of storytelling can motivate people to explore new possibilities, embrace change, and embark on journeys of self-discovery and improvement.

Strategies for eliciting impactful client narratives

Understanding Client Context:

Understanding the client's background, experiences, and context is essential for effective Narrative Coaching. It provides valuable insights into their mindset and challenges, enabling the coach to tailor their approach accordingly.

Questioning Techniques:

Effective questioning techniques help coaches delve deeper into the client's stories, facilitating self-reflection and exploration. Open-ended questions encourage clients to share more detailed narratives, leading to greater insight and understanding.

Active Listening Skills:

Active listening involves giving full attention to the client, understanding their perspective, and empathizing with their emotions. It fosters trust and enhances the coaching relationship, creating a safe space for clients to share their stories openly.

Encouraging Narrative Fluency:

Encouraging clients to express themselves fluidly through stories develops their narrative fluency. This process helps them articulate their thoughts, emotions, and beliefs more coherently, leading to enhanced self-awareness and communication.

Implementing Visualization:

Visualization techniques can enhance storytelling by engaging the client's imagination. It helps them vividly envision their desired outcomes, fostering motivation and clarity in their personal development journey.

Supporting Emotional Expression:

Supporting emotional expression allows clients to explore and process their feelings within their narratives. It aids in catharsis, emotional awareness, and growth, creating a space for clients to address and work through their emotions effectively.

Implementing storytelling techniques in coaching practice

Understanding the client's story is at the core of effective Narrative Coaching. Each person's narrative is a treasure trove of experiences, perceptions, and aspirations that shape their reality. As coaches, creating a safe space for storytelling is paramount. This allows clients to explore their thoughts and feelings openly, fostering a trusting environment where vulnerability is welcomed.

Storytelling serves as a profound tool for self-reflection. Through recounting their experiences, clients gain clarity on their values, motivations, and areas for growth. Techniques for effective storytelling in coaching sessions involve active listening, empathetic responses, and thoughtful questions that guide clients in exploring the depths of their stories.

Metaphors, with their symbolic power, can enrich storytelling by articulating emotions and insights that are sometimes challenging to express directly. Integrating metaphors into clients' narratives can unlock new perspectives and facilitate deeper introspection.

Ethical considerations play a crucial role in storytelling within a coaching context. Respecting client confidentiality, obtaining informed consent before sharing stories, and upholding professional boundaries are vital to maintaining trust and integrity in the coaching relationship. By navigating these ethical aspects thoughtfully, coaches can harness the transformative potential of storytelling to empower clients on their journey of self-discovery and growth.

V. Ethical Considerations in Narrative Coaching

Upholding Professional Standards

Entering the world of narrative coaching requires not only a deep understanding of storytelling and personal growth, but also a commitment to upholding ethical guidelines. As we delve into this crucial aspect of the coaching process, we will explore the importance of respecting client confidentiality, establishing clear boundaries, and navigating potential ethical dilemmas. By recognizing the significance of ethical guidelines, we can ensure that our coaching practices are not only effective, but also ethical and respectful of our clients' stories and trust.

Importance of ethical guidelines in coaching narratives

Ethical guidelines are the cornerstone of narrative coaching, providing coaches with a framework for practicing with integrity and professionalism. These guidelines dictate how coaches should navigate the delicate terrain of client stories, emphasizing respect, sensitivity, and confidentiality. They set a standard for how coaches handle the narratives shared with them, recognizing the deeply personal nature of these stories and the trust placed in the coach-client relationship.

By adhering to ethical guidelines, coaches cultivate an environment of trust and safety, essential for clients to engage authentically in the coaching process. Clients must feel secure in sharing their experiences, knowing that their stories will be handled with discretion and care. This commitment to ethical practices not only honors the client's autonomy but also promotes a deeper level of self-disclosure and vulnerability, crucial for effective coaching outcomes.

Diligence in following ethical guidelines is fundamental to maintaining the professionalism and efficacy of narrative coaching. Coaches who prioritize ethical considerations not only uphold the integrity of the coaching profession but also significantly impact the coaching journey's success. Trust and confidentiality form the bedrock of the coach-client relationship, and ethical guidelines play a pivotal role in preserving these essential components throughout the coaching process. Ultimately, the ethical practice of narrative coaching enhances client outcomes, fostering meaningful personal growth and sustainable change.

Respecting client confidentiality and boundaries

Client confidentiality in coaching is a cornerstone of the coaching relationship, pivotal for engendering trust and facilitating open communication. Upholding confidentiality signifies that a coach must keep all client information strictly confidential, sharing it only with the client's explicit permission. Respecting a client's privacy is not just a professional obligation but a moral imperative in fostering a safe and supportive environment for growth and change.

Establishing and maintaining clear and professional boundaries is essential in coaching relationships. Coaches need to set boundaries regarding communication frequency, response time, session duration, and topics discussed, ensuring a structured and respectful coaching process. It is crucial to differentiate personal feelings from professional responsibilities by prioritizing the client's well-being and maintaining objectivity at all times.

Issues that may arise in maintaining client confidentiality and boundaries include accidental breaches of confidentiality, conflicts of interest, and blurred boundaries due to overpersonalization in the relationship. Coaches must be vigilant in safeguarding client data by securely storing electronic and physical records, using encrypted communication channels, and obtaining written consent before sharing any client information.

In essence, the integrity of the coaching process hinges on the coach's commitment to maintaining confidentiality, establishing clear boundaries, and navigating potential challenges ethically and professionally.

Navigating ethical dilemmas in narrative coaching

Recognizing Ethical Dilemmas in Narrative Coaching is essential for maintaining professionalism and protecting the well-being of clients. Coaches need to be vigilant in identifying complex situations where ethical principles may come into conflict. This may include issues such as dual relationships, conflicts of interest, or breaches of confidentiality.

Managing Power Dynamics is crucial in ensuring a balanced and respectful coaching relationship. Coaches must be mindful of the influence they hold as a trusted confidant and guide, avoiding the misuse of power for personal gain or to manipulate the client's decisions.

Maintaining Confidentiality is a cornerstone of ethical practice in Narrative Coaching. Coaches must uphold strict standards to safeguard the privacy and trust of clients, ensuring that sensitive information shared during coaching sessions remains confidential unless permitted by the client or mandated by law.

Promoting Client Autonomy in Narrative Coaching involves empowering clients to take charge of their own personal development journey. Coaches should encourage self-reflection, decision-making, and goal-setting, while also respecting the client's right to autonomy and self-determination.

Respecting Cultural Differences is essential in a diverse and multicultural coaching landscape. Coaches must embrace cultural humility, sensitivity, and awareness to effectively engage with clients from varying backgrounds, beliefs, and values.

Acting with Integrity is a foundational principle in Narrative Coaching. Coaches are expected to demonstrate honesty, transparency, and ethical conduct in all interactions with clients, colleagues, and stakeholders. Upholding professional standards and ethical guidelines is paramount in building trust and credibility as a Narrative Coach.

Building Trusting Client Relationships

Embarking on a journey of narrative coaching involves more than just listening to stories; it requires a deep understanding of the power dynamics at play. As we delve into this section, we will explore the intricacies of maintaining professional integrity, respecting confidentiality, and navigating the delicate balance of power between coach and client. Let us uncover the importance of creating a safe and empowering environment for clients to share their narratives openly and authentically. Join us in unraveling the complexities of storytelling and the profound impact it has on the coaching relationship.

Cultivating trust through ethical coaching practices

Maintaining the professional integrity of narrative coaching practices hinges on the unwavering commitment to preserving the confidentiality of clients' stories. This imperative requirement underscores the trust placed in the coach by the client, ensuring that their narratives remain safeguarded within the confines of the coaching relationship. Honesty is a cornerstone of this alliance, allowing for transparent and authentic dialogues that serve as the bedrock for productive coaching engagements.

Respectful handling of personal client narratives entails a delicate balance of empathy and professionalism. Coaches must navigate these narratives with sensitivity and compassion, always mindful of the weight and significance of the stories shared. Moreover, a coach's self-awareness and transparency are fundamental to the coaching dynamic, as these qualities bolster trust and foster a safe space for clients to express themselves freely.

Encouraging open and non-judgmental communication forms the cornerstone of effective narrative coaching. By embracing a mindset of empathy and understanding, coaches can create an environment where clients feel valued, heard, and supported in their personal growth and transformation. Upholding these principles elevates the coaching experience, empowering clients to navigate their narratives with courage, resilience, and authenticity.

Addressing power dynamics in storytelling relationships

Power dynamics play a pivotal role in storytelling within a coaching relationship, shaping the narrative and influencing its development. Understanding how power can impact the narrative is crucial for coaches seeking to create a supportive and empowering environment for clients. In this dynamic, coaches hold a significant position of influence, guiding and shaping the client's narrative journey.

Recognizing and acknowledging one's power as a coach is essential in fostering a relationship where the client feels heard and respected. It is paramount to uphold the client's narrative authority, affirming their right to own and control their story. By maintaining a balance in the power dynamics, coaches can ensure that the client's voice remains at the forefront of the storytelling process.

Navigating shifts in power dynamics requires sensitivity and awareness of the evolving nature of the coach-client relationship. Coaches must adapt their approach to accommodate these changes, allowing for a more collaborative and mutually beneficial storytelling experience. To promote an empowering environment, coaches can implement strategies that encourage clients to explore their narratives, fostering growth, self-reflection, and personal development. By fostering a sense of agency and ownership in storytelling, coaches can empower clients to embrace their stories authentically and journey towards transformative change.

Ensuring a safe space for sharing personal narratives

In the practice of Narrative Coaching, one of the foundational elements is the understanding of the client's comfort level in sharing personal narratives. This aspect delves into the client's willingness and readiness to delve into their personal stories, experiences, and emotions. By gauging the client's openness, coaches can tailor their approach to support the client effectively.

Creating a non-judgmental space within the coaching relationship is essential. This environment should be devoid of any biases or prejudices, allowing clients to feel safe and free to explore their narratives without fear of criticism or judgment. Coaches play a critical role in fostering this atmosphere by practicing empathy, active listening, and unconditional positive regard.

Emotional safety is paramount in Narrative Coaching. Coaches must implement mechanisms and strategies to safeguard clients from potential emotional harm that may arise during the coaching process. This could involve setting clear boundaries, offering support systems, and validating the client's emotions to create a safe space for exploration and growth.

Maintaining confidentiality is a cornerstone of ethical coaching practice. Coaches must adhere strictly to policies that protect the client's personal information and ensure that their narratives are kept private and secure. Respecting boundaries is also essential in Narrative Coaching. Coaches should acknowledge and honor the client's personal limits in sharing narratives, being mindful of what the client is comfortable discussing.

Empowering clients and reinforcing their autonomy over their stories is a key principle in Narrative Coaching. By enabling clients to hold control over their narratives, coaches support their agency and self-expression, fostering a sense of ownership and empowerment in the coaching process. This empowerment not only ensures that clients feel in charge of their personal development journey but also cultivates a deeper sense of self-awareness and growth.

VI. Advancing Skills in Narrative Coaching

Mastering Advanced Techniques

Embarking on a journey through the complexities of storytelling, we delve into the art of crafting narratives that resonate deeply with readers. From symbolism and metaphor to non-linear structures, we explore the various elements that contribute to a compelling story. Join us as we analyze the role of perspective, incorporate plot twists, and leverage the power of silence to create suspense and anticipation. Through critical reflection and collaborative co-creation, we navigate emotional content and ethical considerations in narrative analysis. Prepare to embark on a transformative coaching experience, where we uncover the psychological mechanisms behind personal change and implement narrative techniques to measure transformation outcomes.

Exploring nuanced storytelling methods

Understanding intricate story structures involves an artful balance of elements that captivate and engage audiences on multiple levels. Effectively structuring a narrative with emotional resonance requires a delicate interplay of plot development, character arcs, and thematic depth. Symbolism and metaphor serve as the narrative's hidden gems, enriching the storytelling experience by imbuing it with layers of meaning that resonate with the audience's emotions and intellect. By seamlessly integrating symbolic language and metaphors throughout the narrative, storytellers can craft a tapestry of connections that evoke profound insights and provoke thought.

Exploring non-linear narratives offers a fresh perspective on storytelling, allowing for a more dynamic and engaging presentation. By defying traditional chronological order, non-linear narratives challenge both the storyteller and the audience to piece together fragmented events and perspectives, creating a rich tapestry of interconnected moments that offer a deeper understanding of the story's underlying themes and characters.

The role of perspective in storytelling cannot be understated, as it shapes the audience's perception of events and characters. Changing point-of-views within the narrative provides a multifaceted exploration of the story's world, allowing for a more nuanced understanding of its complexities and contradictions.

Incorporating plot twists and suspense adds an element of unpredictability and excitement to the narrative, keeping the audience on the edge of their seats and inviting them to speculate about what might happen next. By strategically introducing unexpected events and revelations, storytellers can create a sense of anticipation and suspense that propels the story forward and deepens the audience's emotional investment in the narrative.

Leveraging silence and pauses within a story is a powerful tool that allows for moments of reflection, tension, and emotional impact. By strategically incorporating silences and pauses at key moments in the narrative, storytellers can create a sense of rhythm and pacing that enhances the overall storytelling experience, allowing for moments of quiet contemplation and emotional resonance to unfold naturally.

Understanding intricate story structures involves a nuanced exploration of the various elements that contribute to a compelling and engaging narrative. By skillfully integrating symbolism and metaphor, exploring non-linear narratives, considering the role of perspective, incorporating plot twists and suspense, and leveraging silence and pauses strategically, storytellers can create narratives that resonate deeply with audiences, leaving a lasting impact long after the story has ended.

Enhancing narrative analysis skills

Narrative analysis plays a crucial role in narrative coaching by unraveling the significance embedded in personal stories. Understanding story structures allows coaches to delve into the core of clients' narratives, identifying patterns, themes, and conflicts that shape their perceptions and behaviors. Through critical reflective skills, coaches can unveil underlying meanings and assumptions within these narratives, offering a deeper understanding and facilitating transformative coaching experiences.

Furthermore, narrative co-creation techniques involve collaborative efforts between the coach and the client to craft new narratives that empower change and growth. This shared storytelling process enhances client engagement and ownership of their personal development journey. Navigating emotional content in narratives demands sensitivity and skill in handling complex emotional stories effectively. Coaches must employ techniques that assist clients in processing and transforming these emotions constructively.

Emphasizing ethical practices and empathy underscores the coach's commitment to creating a safe and trusting space for clients to explore and share their narratives. By embedding these attributes into narrative analysis, coaches uphold professional standards, respect clients' autonomy, and foster a supportive coaching environment conducive to meaningful transformation and growth.

Facilitating transformative coaching experiences

Transformative coaching delves deep into the realm of personal evolution, aiming to catalyze profound shifts in individuals' mindsets and behaviors. Understanding transformative experiences is foundational in this process, recognizing these as pivotal moments of insight, reflection, and growth that propel individuals towards lasting change. Narratives function as powerful tools in personal transformation, enabling individuals to reframe their stories, confront limiting beliefs, and construct narratives that align with their desired outcomes.

Psychological mechanisms underpinning transformation involve intricate processes such as cognitive restructuring, emotional processing, and identity reconstruction. Implementing narrative techniques effectively in transformation encompasses guiding individuals to explore their core narratives, challenge ingrained patterns, and envision new narratives that empower change. The measurement of transformation outcomes is essential for tracking progress and impact, evaluating shifts in beliefs, behaviors, emotional well-being, and overall life satisfaction.

By integrating narrative coaching with transformative principles, coaches can create a space for profound self-reflection, growth, and lasting change. Through a combination of narrative exploration, psychological insight, and measurable outcomes, transformative coaching offers a holistic approach to personal development and empowerment.

Personal Development as a Narrative Coach

Embarking on a journey of self-discovery and growth is a crucial aspect of narrative coaching. As we delve into the realm of personal narratives, we must also recognize the importance of understanding how our own stories can impact our coaching practices. In this section, we will explore the intricacies of recognizing and evolving our personal narratives, the effects of coaching on these narratives, and the transformative power that lies within our own self-reflection. By delving deeper into these concepts, we can not only enhance our coaching skills but also foster a deeper sense of self-awareness that can greatly impact our interactions with clients. Join us on this introspective journey as we navigate the ethical implications and professional growth opportunities that come with embracing our personal narratives in the realm of coaching.

Reflecting on personal growth through coaching practice

Recognizing personal narratives is fundamental in narrative coaching as it involves understanding the stories individuals construct about their lives. These narratives shape our beliefs, behaviors, and perceptions, influencing how we interact with the world and approach challenges. Through coaching, individuals can gain insight into their personal narratives, recognizing patterns, biases, and limitations that may be holding them back or causing distress.

Narrative shifts refer to the transformative changes that can occur in these personal narratives through coaching interventions. By exploring and reshaping these stories, individuals can reframe past experiences, envision new possibilities, and cultivate a more empowering self-concept. This process can lead to increased self-confidence, resilience, and a sense of agency in shaping one's life path.

The effects of coaching on personal narratives are profound, as clients often experience heightened self-awareness, emotional healing, and a clearer sense of purpose. By engaging in reflective exercises, storytelling, and dialogue with their coach, individuals can explore alternative narratives, challenge limiting beliefs, and envision new pathways for personal growth and fulfillment.

Transformation through self-narratives involves embracing the power of storytelling to redefine one's identity, goals, and relationships. By crafting and embodying more empowering narratives, individuals can break free from self-imposed limitations, cultivate resilience, and navigate life transitions with greater confidence and authenticity. Coaching diversity enriches this process by exposing individuals to a variety of perspectives, values, and experiences, fostering empathy, openness, and a deeper understanding of human complexity.

Ethical considerations play a crucial role in guiding personal growth narratives within the coaching relationship. Coaches must uphold confidentiality, respect clients' autonomy, and navigate sensitive topics with empathy and professionalism. By creating a safe and trusting environment, coaches can support clients in exploring and transforming their narratives with integrity and ethical awareness.

Opportunities for ongoing professional development

Ongoing professional growth is critical in narrative coaching as it ensures coaches stay relevant in a rapidly evolving field by embracing new methodologies and perspectives. By becoming members of professional coaching associations, coaches gain access to a vast array of resources, including workshops, conferences, and networking opportunities that facilitate continued learning. Active involvement in such associations fosters a vibrant community where coaches can exchange ideas, share experiences, and stay informed about emerging industry trends.

Regular participation in professional development activities is a cornerstone of staying abreast of the latest narrative coaching approaches and strategies. Engaging in workshops, seminars, and training sessions not only broadens a coach's skill set but also provides fresh insights that can infuse coaching sessions with renewed vigor and efficacy.

Self-reflection plays a pivotal role in narrative coaching, as coaches who actively work on improving their own narratives can better empathize with and guide clients through their personal stories. By unraveling and reconstructing their own narratives, coaches deepen their understanding of human behavior and enhance their ability to facilitate transformative change in clients.

Furthermore, the guidance and support from senior coaches or mentors are invaluable for fostering continuous improvement. These experienced professionals offer constructive feedback, share best practices, and serve as role models, inspiring emerging coaches to refine their craft and navigate challenges effectively.

Emphasizing the importance of regularly updating their understanding of professional ethics, narrative coaches ensure they uphold the highest standards of practice. By staying attuned to ethical guidelines and principles, coaches safeguard the integrity of their coaching relationships and cultivate a culture of trust and respect.

In essence, committing to ongoing professional growth through membership in coaching associations, active participation in development activities, self-reflection, mentorship, and ethical diligence is not only crucial for narrative coaches but also enriches the coaching experience for both practitioners and clients alike.

Integrating self-awareness into coaching approaches

Self-awareness stands as a fundamental pillar in coaching, encompassing a profound comprehension of one's inner workings. It revolves around recognizing one's emotions, thoughts, and behavioral patterns, alongside acknowledging personal strengths, weaknesses, values, and beliefs that inherently shape coaching interactions. In the coaching realm, self-awareness profoundly impacts client relationships, fostering empathetic connections, emotional regulation, and fluid communication channels. Coaches adept in self-awareness are poised to adapt their coaching strategies to cater to individual client needs, ensuring a bespoke and effective coaching experience.

The monitoring and enhancement of self-awareness within coaching practice necessitate ongoing introspection, soliciting feedback, and engaging in self-assessment to refine coaching efficacy continually. Ethical considerations surrounding self-awareness delve into acknowledging and managing personal biases, steering clear of judgmental attitudes, and upholding unwavering objectivity to orchestrate coaching sessions founded on fairness and reverence. In navigating the complex terrain of coaching, integrating self-awareness not only enriches the coach's proficiency but also substantiates the transformative potential of the coaching relationship for profound client growth and development.

VII. Reinforcing Narrative Coaching Practices

Resources for Continued Learning

Embarking on a journey of continuous growth and development in the field of narrative coaching involves a multifaceted approach. From exploring advanced courses to engaging in research and publications, each step taken plays a pivotal role in honing your skills and staying abreast of the latest trends and techniques. In this section, we will delve into the various aspects of post-graduate degree programs, workshops, online platforms, supervision, and community networking that contribute to your professional growth in narrative coaching. Let's navigate through the avenues that pave the way for your continued success in this dynamic field.

Further training opportunities in narrative coaching

Advanced post-graduate degree programs in narrative coaching provide a comprehensive exploration of this dynamic field, delving deeply into advanced courses that focus on honing specialized techniques and strategies. E-learning platforms offer a convenient avenue for individuals seeking certified courses in narrative coaching, catering to diverse learning preferences and schedules. Participation in workshops and seminars, both at local and international levels, serves as a valuable opportunity to immerse oneself in the practical application of narrative coaching principles and connect with like-minded professionals.

Supervision, whether through peer or professional settings, acts as a crucial component in the advancement of narrative coaching skills, offering valuable feedback and guidance for ongoing development. Membership in narrative coaching associations not only fosters a sense of community but also provides access to a network of experienced practitioners, opening doors for collaboration and mentorship opportunities.

Engaging in research initiatives and contributing to publications within the field serves as a means of staying abreast of emerging trends and contributing to the collective knowledge base of narrative coaching. By actively involving oneself in research and publishing endeavors, individuals not only enhance their own understanding but also contribute to the ongoing growth and evolution of narrative coaching practices.

Continuing education options for narrative coaches

Staying updated with new techniques and theories in narrative coaching is essential for coaches to remain effective and relevant in their practice. Formal education provides a structured environment for in-depth learning and understanding of foundational principles, allowing coaches to cultivate a strong theoretical framework to guide their interventions. Workshops and seminars offer practical insights and hands-on experience, enabling coaches to integrate new approaches into their practice in a dynamic and interactive setting.

Online learning platforms provide convenient access to a wealth of resources, including webinars, courses, and research materials, allowing coaches to stay informed about the latest trends and developments in narrative coaching. Peer learning and networking opportunities create a space for coaches to exchange ideas, share experiences, and collaborate with colleagues, fostering a community of learning and continuous improvement.

Furthermore, a focus on ethics and professional development ensures that coaches uphold standards of accountability, confidentiality, and respect in their interactions with clients, maintaining trust and integrity in the coaching relationship. By embracing ongoing learning and growth, coaches can enhance their skills, expand their knowledge base, and ultimately offer more impactful support to their clients on their journey of personal development and change.

Building a supportive community of narrative coaching professionals

Understanding the importance of community within professional spheres is paramount for individual and collective advancement. By actively seeking and engaging in community networks, professionals can access a wealth of resources, knowledge, and support. These networks provide a platform for sharing best practices, exchanging ideas, and fostering collaboration.

Participating in peer review processes is not only a way to contribute to the field's quality standards but also an opportunity for personal growth and learning. Through constructive feedback and dialogue with peers, professionals can refine their skills, receive valuable insights, and enhance their understanding of best practices.

Supporting professional development within a community involves not only seeking growth opportunities for oneself but also facilitating growth for others. This can take the form of mentorship, knowledge sharing, and creating a supportive environment for continuous learning.

Adhering to our responsibilities within the community means upholding ethical standards, respecting diversity, and promoting a culture of inclusivity and mutual respect. By fulfilling our obligations to the community, we contribute to a positive and collaborative environment where all members can thrive.

In essence, active participation in community networks, sharing best practices, engaging in peer review, supporting professional development, and upholding responsibilities are key pillars for personal and collective growth within professional communities. By embracing these principles, professionals can foster a culture of continuous improvement, collaboration, and excellence.

Future Trends in Narrative Coaching

As we delve into the realm of technological advancements and their impact on narrative coaching, a new world of possibilities unveils itself. From the integration of virtual reality to the role of artificial intelligence, these advancements are reshaping the way stories are told and shared in coaching practices. Join us on a journey through the influence of neuroscience discoveries, the emergence of communal narratives, and the evolution of ethical considerations as we explore the ever-expanding horizons of narrative coaching in the digital age.

Emerging developments in narrative coaching

The influence of neurosciences on storytelling techniques in coaching has revolutionized the understanding of how narratives impact individuals at a neural level. Insights from neuroscience have shown how storytelling can evoke emotional responses, strengthen memory retention, and even influence decision-making processes. By incorporating this knowledge into narrative coaching, practitioners can tailor storytelling techniques to better engage clients, enhance learning, and stimulate positive change.

Integration of technology in narrative coaching has ushered in a new era of innovation and efficiency in the coaching process. From virtual reality experiences to digital story creation platforms, technological tools offer coaches the means to deliver impactful sessions, track progress, and provide clients with personalized resources for continued growth. Technology also enables remote coaching sessions, making coaching more accessible to individuals who may not have otherwise been able to participate.

Diversity and inclusion in narrative coaching are essential components for creating a supportive and empowering coaching environment. Embracing diverse narratives and perspectives enriches the coaching experience, fosters greater empathy, and helps break down barriers to inclusion. By recognizing and valuing the unique stories of each individual, coaches can create a safe space for exploration, growth, and transformation.

The rise of collective narratives in coaching emphasizes the power of shared stories and communal experiences in driving personal and collective growth.

By recognizing the interconnected nature of our stories, individuals can find common ground, build empathy, and work together towards common goals. Collective narratives foster a sense of community and belonging, providing individuals with a support network that encourages collaboration and mutual understanding.

The emergence of ecological narratives in coaching highlights the interconnectedness between personal narratives and the broader environmental context. By expanding the scope of storytelling to include relationships with the natural world, coaches can help clients develop a deeper sense of environmental responsibility, mindfulness, and interconnectedness. Ecological narratives encourage individuals to consider the impact of their stories on the world around them, fostering a more holistic approach to personal development and change.

Expanding research in narrative coaching is vital for advancing the field and enhancing the efficacy of coaching interventions. Rigorous research studies provide evidence-based insights into the effectiveness of narrative coaching techniques, helping to validate its impact on personal development and change. By continuously expanding research efforts, the field of narrative coaching can evolve, innovate, and stay at the forefront of evidence-based coaching practices.

The integration of neurosciences, technology, diversity, collective narratives, ecological perspectives, and ongoing research in narrative coaching is shaping the future of coaching practices. By harnessing the power of stories in innovative ways, coaches can help individuals navigate personal challenges, foster growth, and embark on transformative journeys towards self-discovery and positive change.

Innovations shaping the future of narrative coaching

Technology has revolutionized the landscape of narrative coaching, offering unprecedented opportunities for coaches and clients alike. Virtual reality (VR) presents a powerful tool for enhancing the coaching experience, allowing individuals to immerse themselves in personalized narratives that facilitate self-reflection and growth. By leveraging VR, coaches can create engaging and transformative storytelling environments that help clients explore their identities and address challenges in a deeply impactful way.

Artificial intelligence (AI) is another technological advancement that is reshaping narrative coaching. AI systems can analyze vast amounts of data to identify patterns in clients' narratives, providing valuable insights that can inform coaching strategies and interventions. Additionally, AI-powered tools can aid in the creation of personalized coaching programs tailored to the specific needs and goals of individual clients, enhancing the effectiveness of the coaching process.

Moreover, neuroscience discoveries have shed light on the intricate workings of neuronal story networks in the brain, highlighting the neurobiological basis of storytelling and its profound influence on personal development. By understanding how stories shape our thoughts, emotions, and behaviors, coaches can leverage this knowledge to facilitate meaningful and lasting change in their clients.

Social media platforms have also played a significant role in shaping communal narratives and collective storytelling in the context of coaching. By engaging with online communities and sharing stories and experiences, individuals can connect with others, gain diverse perspectives, and learn from a wide range of narratives, enriching their own coaching journey.

As technology continues to advance, coaches must remain vigilant in navigating the ethical considerations that accompany these new narrative coaching practices. From ensuring client confidentiality and privacy in the digital age to addressing potential biases in AI algorithms, coaches must stay attuned to the evolving ethical landscape and uphold professional standards to maintain trust and integrity in their coaching relationships.

Recommendations for staying current in the field

Embrace Continuous Learning:

To stay relevant and impactful, it is crucial for narrative coaches to commit to lifelong learning and growth in their field. This includes staying updated on the latest trends, research, and innovations within narrative coaching.

Follow Key Thought-Leaders in Narrative Coaching:

To expand knowledge and gain new insights, it is beneficial to follow influential figures in narrative coaching through their writings, talks, and workshops. This can provide fresh perspectives and ideas for enhancing coaching practices.

Connect with Industry Peers:

Building a network of fellow narrative coaches fosters collaboration, support, and the exchange of ideas. Connecting with industry peers allows for sharing experiences and learning from each other's successes and challenges.

Update Coaching Technique Portfolio:

Regularly refining and diversifying coaching techniques ensures adaptability and effectiveness in client interactions. Adding new tools and approaches to the coaching toolkit enhances the ability to tailor sessions to individual client needs.

Active Participation in Coaching Associations:

Involvement in coaching associations facilitates professional development, networking opportunities, and access to resources. Active participation in such communities can contribute to staying informed, connected, and supported in the coaching profession.

Engaging in Regular Self-Reflection:

Personal growth and effectiveness as a coach are nurtured through regular self-reflection and introspection. This practice promotes awareness, authenticity, and continuous improvement in coaching approaches and interactions.

VIII. Concluding Thoughts and Application of Narrative Coaching

Summary of Key Insights

Embarking on a journey through the world of narrative coaching, we unravel the intricate ways in which stories shape our identities and actions. From understanding the diverse types of stories utilized in coaching to mastering techniques that cultivate personal change, this section delves into the transformative power of narratives in personal and professional growth. Explore the ethical considerations, continuous learning opportunities, and the creation of safe spaces necessary for fostering personal insight, overcoming limiting beliefs, boosting effectiveness, and transforming relationships. Join us as we navigate the terrain of narrative coaching and discover the profound impact of storytelling in unleashing potential and igniting change.

Recap of core concepts in narrative coaching

Narrative coaching delves into the profound influence stories have on our identities and actions, recognizing them as powerful tools for personal development. By identifying various types of stories—

such as success narratives, self-limiting beliefs, or pivotal life events—coaches can tailor their approach to support clients effectively. These stories serve as mirrors reflecting individuals' inner worlds and beliefs, offering valuable insights for growth.

Narrative coaching techniques equip coaches with the ability to reframe narratives, shifting perspectives and unlocking new possibilities for clients. By guiding individuals to explore and reconstruct their personal narratives, coaches facilitate transformative change and empower clients to actively shape their future.

Ethical considerations play a crucial role in narrative coaching, emphasizing the need to honor and protect clients' stories with utmost respect and confidentiality. Building a safe and trusting space for clients to share and navigate their narratives fosters a foundation for meaningful progress and personal growth.

Continuous learning in narrative coaching is essential for coaches to refine their skills, stay updated on best practices, and adapt to evolving client needs. Emphasizing ongoing professional development ensures that coaches can effectively leverage the power of storytelling to catalyze lasting change and support clients on their journey towards self-discovery and personal fulfillment.

Highlights from successful narrative coaching applications

Finding Personal Insight:

Narrative Coaching serves as a powerful tool for individuals seeking personal insight. By delving into their narratives, individuals can uncover subtle nuances, hidden motivations, and underlying patterns that shape their beliefs and behaviors. Through this process, they gain a deeper understanding of themselves, their values, and their aspirations, leading to enhanced self-awareness and personal growth.

Overcoming Limiting Beliefs:

Limiting beliefs can significantly hinder personal development and success. Narrative Coaching provides a structured approach for individuals to identify, challenge, and reframe these beliefs. By examining the stories they tell themselves, individuals can break free from self-imposed limitations, build resilience, and cultivate a more empowering narrative that aligns with their true potential and goals.

Boosting Personal Effectiveness:

Narrative Coaching empowers individuals to boost their personal effectiveness by aligning their actions with their core values and aspirations. By crafting narratives that reflect their authentic selves and desired outcomes, individuals can gain clarity, focus, and motivation to make meaningful progress in their personal and professional lives.

Transforming Relationship Dynamics:

Narrative Coaching plays a vital role in transforming relationship dynamics by encouraging individuals to explore the stories they carry within their interactions. By fostering empathy, understanding, and effective communication, individuals can reshape their narratives to build stronger, more meaningful connections with others, leading to healthier and more fulfilling relationships.

Fostering Personal Growth:

Through narrative exploration and reflective storytelling, Narrative Coaching facilitates personal growth by helping individuals embrace change, learn from past experiences, and adapt to new challenges. By embracing their stories as a source of learning and growth, individuals can cultivate resilience, enhance self-efficacy, and step into their full potential with confidence and purpose.

Application in Professional Settings:

In professional settings, Narrative Coaching offers a unique approach to personal and professional development. By leveraging storytelling techniques, individuals can enhance their leadership skills, navigate career transitions, and cultivate a growth mindset that fosters continuous learning and innovation. Moreover, Narrative Coaching can improve communication, foster authentic connections, and promote a culture of trust and collaboration within organizations, ultimately leading to enhanced performance, job satisfaction, and overall success in the workplace.

Key takeaways for implementing narrative coaching strategies

Creating a safe space in Narrative Coaching is paramount for the transformative journey of clients. It involves establishing an environment where individuals feel comfortable to share their stories authentically and without judgment. As coaches, honing our listening skills is crucial in this process. Active listening not only helps us comprehend the narratives shared but also demonstrates our empathy and commitment to understanding the client's unique perspective. Through attentive listening, coaches can offer valuable insights and reflections that aid clients in gaining clarity and self-awareness.

Selecting apt stories is another vital aspect of Narrative Coaching. Stories serve as a powerful tool for connecting with the client's emotions and experiences, facilitating introspection and growth. Coaches must carefully choose narratives that resonate with the client's challenges and aspirations, sparking meaningful reflections and insights.

Cultivating narrative intelligence is about developing a deeper understanding of the stories we encounter—both our clients' narratives and our own. It involves deciphering the underlying themes, beliefs, and emotions interwoven within the stories shared. By honing this skill, coaches can guide clients in exploring their stories more profoundly, uncovering hidden patterns, and transforming limiting beliefs.

Ethical conduct is a cornerstone of Narrative Coaching. Respecting clients' confidentiality, privacy, and autonomy is non-negotiable. Coaches must uphold strict ethical standards, ensuring that clients' stories are handled with care and respect throughout the coaching journey.

A commitment to continued learning is essential for Narrative Coaches to evolve and enhance their practice continually. Staying abreast of emerging trends, theories, and techniques in the field allows coaches to offer innovative and effective coaching experiences. By investing in ongoing professional development, coaches can expand their knowledge base, refine their skills, and deliver exceptional results for their clients.

Encouragement for Practical Implementation

Join me on a journey through the transformative power of personal narratives. In this section, we will delve into the world of narrative coaching and explore how stories drive personal and professional growth. From understanding the effectiveness of narrative coaching to showcasing real-life examples of transformation, we will uncover the emotional and cognitive advantages of using stories in coaching. Together, we will learn how to tailor coaching techniques by gaining insights into clients' narratives, encouraging storytelling, and utilizing active listening. Let's explore the ethical responsibilities and professional growth that come with leveraging the power of personal stories for self-realization and development.

Motivation to apply narrative coaching techniques

Narrative coaching is a powerful tool for driving personal and professional growth by harnessing the transformative potential of storytelling. By engaging with clients' narratives, coaches create a safe space for exploration, reflection, and change. This method allows individuals to gain a deeper understanding of themselves, their values, and their aspirations, leading to enhanced self-awareness and personal development.

The effectiveness of narrative coaching lies in its ability to tap into both the emotional and cognitive aspects of human experience. Stories evoke empathy, help individuals make sense of their experiences, and stimulate creativity, fostering resilience and problem-solving skills. Through narrative coaching, clients can reframe their narratives, challenge limiting beliefs, and envision new possibilities for themselves.

Real-life examples abound in showcasing the impact of narrative coaching in enabling transformation. Clients have been able to navigate career transitions, improve relationships, and overcome personal obstacles by leveraging the power of storytelling to explore their inner worlds and make positive changes in their lives.

The applicability of narrative coaching extends across various contexts, from career development to personal growth, making it a versatile approach for fostering change and growth. Its emphasis on continual learning and skill development underscores the importance of ongoing self-reflection and narrative exploration in promoting personal and professional evolution.

Moreover, ethical responsibility and professional growth are core tenets of narrative coaching. Coaches must uphold confidentiality, respect clients' stories, and adhere to ethical standards while also focusing on their own development to enhance their coaching effectiveness. By integrating narrative coaching into their practice, coaches can not only support their clients' growth but also deepen their own skills and expertise in guiding transformative journeys through the power of stories.

Actionable steps for incorporating storytelling into coaching practice

Understanding Clients' Stories:

In the realm of Narrative Coaching, delving into clients' stories serves as a cornerstone for tailoring coaching techniques to suit individual needs effectively. By understanding the narratives that clients bring forth, coaches can grasp the intricacies of their experiences, perspectives, and aspirations. This comprehension allows coaches to personalize their approaches, addressing clients' unique challenges and goals with greater precision and empathy.

Encouraging Storytelling:

Encouraging clients to share their stories within the coaching space is pivotal for fostering self-expression and self-discovery. Through storytelling, clients can articulate their inner thoughts, emotions, and life experiences, facilitating a deeper exploration of their personal narratives. This process aids clients in gaining clarity, insight, and a sense of ownership over their stories, empowering them to navigate challenges, set meaningful goals, and embark on transformative journeys of personal growth.

Utilizing Active Listening:

Active listening stands as a fundamental practice in Narrative Coaching, enabling coaches to engage fully with the client's story and demonstrate genuine care and attentiveness. By attentively listening to both the spoken words and the underlying emotions and nuances within the narrative, coaches can glean valuable insights into clients' perspectives, values, and aspirations. This active engagement fosters trust, rapport, and mutual understanding, laying a solid foundation for fruitful coaching interactions and transformative outcomes.

Embedding Storytelling in Coaching Sessions:

By integrating storytelling as a regular activity in coaching sessions, coaches create a dynamic platform for clients to explore, reflect on, and reshape their narratives continually. With storytelling woven into the fabric of coaching sessions, clients are prompted to engage in introspection, self-discovery, and goal-setting, fostering a culture of ongoing growth and development. This practice invites clients to embrace their narratives as vehicles for empowerment and transformation, cultivating resilience, self-awareness, and a sense of agency in their personal and professional lives.

Analyzing Stories for Coaching Insights:

Through a thoughtful analysis of clients' narratives, coaches can uncover underlying patterns, beliefs, and opportunities for growth and development. By examining the themes, conflicts, and resolutions within clients' stories, coaches can identify recurring patterns, limiting beliefs, and potential areas for exploration and transformation. This analytical process equips coaches with valuable insights and perspectives, guiding them in tailoring coaching interventions, setting goals, and supporting clients in their quest for personal and professional fulfillment.

Respecting and Managing Story Confidentiality:

In the practice of Narrative Coaching, upholding the principles of ethics, confidentiality, and professional boundaries is crucial for maintaining trust, respect, and integrity. Coaches are entrusted with the sensitive and personal narratives of their clients, necessitating a high level of discretion and confidentiality in handling these stories. By ethically safeguarding clients' narrative privacy, coaches honor the sacredness of their stories, creating a safe and supportive environment for exploration, growth, and transformation within the coaching relationship. This commitment to ethical practice not only upholds professional standards but also nurtures a culture of trust, collaboration, and empowerment in the coaching partnership.

Inspiring clients towards personal growth and transformation

Personal narratives are the building blocks of self-realization and development within the narrative coaching framework. These stories, shaped by individual experiences, emotions, and beliefs, provide a pathway for clients to explore their identities, confront their fears, and envision new possibilities. By fostering safe and non-judgmental spaces, coaches enable clients to share their narratives authentically, leading to moments of profound insight and growth. The act of listening with empathy is paramount in this process, as it cultivates deep understanding and a sense of connection between the coach and the client, propelling the individual towards positive change.

In utilizing narrative coaching to navigate life's challenges, clients are encouraged to reframe their stories, identify recurring themes, and envision alternative endings. This process allows for a deeper understanding of one's inner world and external circumstances, empowering individuals to navigate obstacles with resilience and clarity. Coaches must uphold ethical standards by respecting the sensitivity and confidentiality of clients' stories, ensuring a foundation of trust and safety.

Ultimately, the intertwining of personal narratives and narrative coaching offers a transformative journey towards self-discovery, growth, and empowerment. By embracing the power of storytelling, individuals can embark on a path of personal evolution guided by empathy, introspection, and resilience.

IX. Supplemental Materials and Resources

Glossary of Essential Terms

As you delve into the world of narrative coaching, you will explore the power of personal stories and the impact they have on coaching relationships. Through storytelling techniques and ethical practices, you will learn how to uncover and re-author narratives for personal development and transformation. By understanding the concept of dominant narratives and the importance of ethical considerations, you will navigate the complexities of coaching with respect and integrity. Join me as we unravel the intricacies of narrative coaching and its potential for profound change.

Definition and explanation of key narrative coaching terms

Narrative coaching is a transformative approach that delves into the power of personal stories to facilitate growth and change. In this method, coaches guide clients to explore and reframe their narratives, beliefs, and experiences, leading to enhanced self-awareness and positive transformation. By engaging with personal narratives, individuals gain insights into their identities, values, and behaviors, paving the way for profound personal development.

Personal narratives, the stories we tell ourselves about our lives, significantly influence how we perceive the world and ourselves. In narrative coaching, these narratives are thoroughly examined and reconstructed to foster new perspectives and avenues for personal growth. This process helps clients understand the impact of their stories, identify limiting beliefs, and construct empowering narratives that align with their aspirations and values.

Storytelling techniques are core elements of narrative coaching, encompassing the use of metaphors, anecdotes, and reflective narratives to facilitate introspection, emotional connection, and cognitive reframing. Through skillful storytelling, coaches can guide clients towards a deeper understanding of their experiences, emotions, and aspirations, enabling them to navigate challenges and achieve desired outcomes effectively.

Ethical considerations are paramount in narrative coaching, emphasizing the coach's commitment to confidentiality, respect for clients' autonomy, and the establishment of a trusting and safe coaching environment. Coaches must uphold ethical standards, ensure clear boundaries, and prioritize the well-being and autonomy of their clients throughout the coaching process. By embedding ethics into their practice, narrative coaches can uphold the integrity and effectiveness of the coaching relationship, fostering meaningful and sustainable personal development for their clients.

Clarifying terminology for effective communication in coaching

Narrative Coaching is a specialized approach that delves into the power of personal stories for fostering personal development and catalyzing change. Unlike traditional coaching methods, Narrative Coaching places significant emphasis on the influence of narratives in shaping an individual's sense of self and their capacity for growth. Central to this approach is the concept of the Dominant Narrative, which denotes the overarching storyline that individuals adhere to, impacting their beliefs, behaviors, and perceptions of themselves and their circumstances.

Within the realm of Narrative Coaching, establishing a robust coaching alliance, defining a clear coaching contract, and respecting healthy boundaries are essential components for cultivating a supportive and effective coaching relationship. Through the practice of 'story-mining,' coaches can effectively extract and explore the narratives that lie at the core of their clients' experiences, thereby unearthing valuable insights and fostering meaningful personal transformations.

One of the key tools employed in Narrative Coaching is 're-authoring,' a technique that involves revisiting and reshaping dominant narratives to empower clients, unlock new perspectives, and facilitate profound personal growth. Upholding ethical standards is paramount in Narrative Coaching, which entails honoring client confidentiality, setting and maintaining respectful boundaries, and upholding professional integrity throughout the coaching journey. By adhering to these principles and practices, Narrative Coaches can guide their clients towards transformative self-discovery and sustainable positive change.

Enhancing understanding through a comprehensive glossary

Definition of Narrative Coaching:

Narrative coaching is a transformative approach that harnesses the power of storytelling to inspire personal growth and change. It involves understanding and reshaping the stories individuals tell themselves about their lives, fostering self-awareness and empowering them to rewrite their narratives in ways that align with their goals and values.

Story-Based Methods in Coaching:

In narrative coaching, stories serve as the foundation for exploration and discovery. Coaches help clients identify and understand the narratives that shape their identities and beliefs. By delving into these stories, clients gain fresh insights into their challenges, emotions, and aspirations, paving the way for transformative change.

Narrative Thinking versus Traditional Coaching:

Unlike traditional coaching approaches that often focus on goal-setting and problem-solving, narrative coaching delves deeply into the stories individuals construct about their lives and explores how these stories influence their perceptions, choices, and behaviors. By recognizing and reframing these narratives, clients can unlock new possibilities for growth and development.

Interpreting Narratives in Coaching:

Coaches in narrative coaching skillfully interpret clients' narratives to uncover hidden meanings, recurring themes, and areas for exploration. By engaging with these narratives, coaches can help clients make sense of their experiences, gain clarity on their values and beliefs, and envision new paths forward.

Understanding Coaching Relationship Dynamics:

In narrative coaching, the coaching relationship is central to the process of personal transformation. Coaches establish a foundation of trust, empathy, and openness, creating a safe space for clients to share their stories authentically. By cultivating a strong coaching relationship, coaches can support clients in navigating their narratives and effecting meaningful change.

Ethical Responsibilities in Narrative Coaching:

Ethics play a crucial role in narrative coaching, guiding coaches in maintaining the integrity and confidentiality of clients' stories. Coaches must uphold professional standards, respect clients' autonomy and boundaries, and handle sensitive information with discretion and sensitivity. By adhering to ethical principles, coaches honor the trust placed in them and uphold the values of integrity and respect in the coaching relationship.

Further Reading and Professional Networks

Embark on a journey through the world of coaching associations, where like-minded professionals come together to grow, learn, and thrive. Discover the significance of these organizations, explore the benefits of membership, and unlock a wealth of resources to enhance your coaching practice. Join us as we delve into the realm of narrative coaching associations, connecting with fellow coaches, sharing experiences, and fostering collaborative relationships. Learn how to navigate ethical standards, pursue educational opportunities, and stay informed on industry trends. Let's dive in and harness the power of community and professional development in the world of narrative coaching.

Recommending additional resources for in-depth learning

Relevant Books:

For in-depth exploration in Narrative Coaching, consider "The Power of Storytelling: Captivate, Convince, or Convert Any Business Audience Using Stories from Top CEOs" by Jim Holtje, offering insights into the persuasive power of narratives in professional settings. Additionally, "Narrative Coaching: The Definitive Guide to Bringing New Stories to Life" by David B. Drake provides a comprehensive framework for incorporating storytelling in coaching practice, aiding personal development and transformative change.

Renowned Authors:

Delve into the works of notable authors such as David B. Drake, acclaimed for his expertise in Narrative Coaching methodologies. Dr. David R. Peterson, a respected figure in the coaching field, offers valuable perspectives on narrative-based approaches. David Emerald is another influential author known for contributions to the field of narrative thinking and transformative coaching techniques.

Relevant Research Papers:

Explore insightful research papers like "The Role of Narratives in Change Processes" by Emma Bell, shedding light on the significance of stories in effecting change. Equally valuable is "The Power of Stories: A Guide for Coaches and Leaders" by John Eisner, emphasizing the impactful role narratives play in coaching and leadership contexts.

E-learning Platforms:

Expand your knowledge through platforms like Udemy, offering courses on Narrative Coaching fundamentals. Coursera provides access to specialized coaching programs, while platforms like Coacharya offer interactive e-learning experiences tailored to coaching professionals.

Professional Networks:

Engage with professional networks such as the International Coach Federation (ICF) and the European Mentoring and Coaching Council (EMCC) for industry insights and networking opportunities. The Association for Coaching serves as another valuable resource for connecting with coaching professionals worldwide.

Conferences and Webinars:

Participate in industry events like the International Coach Federation Global Conference, an enriching platform for knowledge exchange and professional development. The World Business and Executive Coach Summit (WBECS) offers access to top industry speakers and thought leaders. Additionally, consider attending the Center for Narrative Coaching and Leadership (CNCL) Annual Institute for immersive workshops and webinars on narrative coaching practices and advancements.

Directory of coaching associations and organizations

Coaching associations serve as vital pillars in the coaching industry, offering a myriad of benefits crucial for professional growth and success. Among the globally recognized organizations, the International Coach Federation (ICF) stands as a leading authority, setting standards for coaching excellence worldwide. The European Mentoring and Coaching Council (EMCC) and the Association for Coaching (AC) also hold significant influence in their respective regions.

Members of these associations gain access to a treasure trove of resources, from educational materials to exclusive networking opportunities. The perks extend to discounts on conferences, workshops, and courses, bolstering continuous professional development. The process to join typically involves submitting an application, paying membership fees, and agreeing to uphold the association's ethics and guidelines.

Ethical standards are paramount within these associations. Members are expected to adhere to robust codes of conduct, ensuring integrity and respect in their coaching practice.

One of the primary draws of membership lies in the educational and certification opportunities offered by these organizations. They provide a range of courses and accreditation programs, equipping coaches with the knowledge and credentials essential for a successful coaching career.

Embarking on this membership journey involves researching and selecting the association that aligns most closely with your coaching philosophy and goals. As you navigate the landscape of coaching associations, consider the unique offerings and values of each, as they play a significant role in shaping your professional trajectory.

Building connections within the narrative coaching community

Understanding the narrative coaching community is essential for narrative coaches seeking to expand their professional network and enhance their skills. Key narrative coaching associations such as the International Coach Federation (ICF) and the Association for Coaching (AC) offer valuable resources, networking opportunities, and professional development support. Engaging with these associations allows coaches to connect with like-minded individuals, share best practices, and stay updated on industry trends.

Networking with other narrative coaches provides a platform for collaborative learning and the exchange of insights, challenges, and innovations. By building relationships within the narrative coaching community, coaches can gain diverse perspectives, receive feedback, and establish potential partnerships for joint projects or initiatives.

To join narrative coaching associations, individuals can follow guidelines outlined on the associations' websites and explore membership options that best suit their needs. Utilizing professional networking platforms like LinkedIn offers a convenient way to connect with narrative coaches globally, share content, and engage in discussions within relevant groups or forums.

Maintaining active participation in narrative coaching events, such as conferences, workshops, and online forums, is crucial for staying abreast of industry developments and expanding one's professional network. By actively engaging in these events, coaches can enhance their knowledge, gain exposure to new ideas, and establish meaningful connections with peers and industry experts.

Continuing education plays a pivotal role in professional growth within the narrative coaching field. Pursuing ongoing learning opportunities, such as advanced training programs, workshops, and webinars, is essential for staying current with emerging trends, honing coaching skills, and enriching one's coaching practice. By prioritizing continuous education and professional development, narrative coaches can elevate their expertise, serve their clients effectively, and contribute to the advancement of the narrative coaching profession.